SEYMOUR, A GIBBON

SEYMOUR, A GIBBON

About Apes and
Other Animals and
How You Can
Help to Keep
Them Alive

PHYLLIS BOREA

PHOTOGRAPHS BY

RAIMONDO BOREA

FOREWORD BY DUANE M. RUMBAUGH, PH.D.

A MARGARET K. MCELDERRY BOOK

Atheneum 1973 New York

To Roberto and Carla
who introduced us to Seymour
and his friends

Copyright © 1973 by Raimondo and Phyllis Borea
All rights reserved
Library of Congress catalog card number 73–75431
ISBN 0–689–30415–3
Published simultaneously in Canada by McClelland and Stewart, Ltd.
Manufactured in the United States of America
Printed by Halliday Lithograph Corporation
West Hanover, Massachusetts
Bound by A. Horowitz & Son/Bookbinders
Clifton, New Jersey
Designed by Harriett Barton
First Edition

Foreword

If Mother Nature has a sense of beauty, then she must truly love gibbons. Gibbons are poetry in motion. They have taught me and others a great deal about animal life and about man, himself. Delicate and petite, their appearance provides sharp contrast with the other apes—the great apes, all of which are quite large, massive, and powerful.

Gibbons move in fascinating ways. When on the ground, they frequently walk erect on their legs, as though they were men. When they do so, they can touch the ground, for their slender arms are very long. Their arms are not particularly strong, but they are, nonetheless, perfectly designed for brachiating (moving hand over hand) through the treetops and for taking long, breathtaking "flights" through the air of perhaps as much as 50 feet! Their erect, bipedal (two-legged) walk on the ground reminds us of ourselves; their brachiation through the trees makes us stop and wonder—were our primitive ancestors at all like the gibbons of today?

Though tender and loving while young, just as the best of human babies are expected to be, adult gibbons are inevitably of a different temperament—volatile, unpredictable, and often very dangerous. My family and I have seen two infant gibbons grow up to adulthood. It pained us to see them change, to see them become untrustworthy. We continued to care for them, but from afar, and, somehow, we believed that they, too, continued to care for us just as they had when they were young. The bond of affection was never broken, but both we and they knew that things had changed. As adults, they were what their nature ultimately dictated.

Man should be able to enjoy gibbons, but it is unwise and unfair for him to have them as household pets. Gibbons in captivity should have large exercise areas and as much freedom as can be provided, for they, and all other wildlife, are meant to be free, to live with their own. As humans we must work to ensure the survival of gibbons, and all animals, not just for ourselves and not just for the pleasure of generations of children yet unborn, but for the animals themselves. They have every right to share life in the world with us.

In this book the author and the photographer provide an exciting and accurate description of gibbons and, through them, a fine introduction to the study of primates. They provide, as well, interesting suggestions for readers who would like to share in the protection and preservation of animals.

Duane M. Rumbaugh

CHAIRMAN AND PROFESSOR
DEPARTMENT OF PSYCHOLOGY
GEORGIA STATE UNIVERSITY
AND
COLLABORATING SCIENTIST
YERKES PRIMATE RESEARCH CENTER
ATLANTA, GEORGIA

SEYMOUR, A GIBBON

PART ONE

What kind of hand is this? What is it reaching for? To whom does it belong?

And it is a hand, not a paw. It can pat a cheek. Or pull a handful of hair. It gets its owner into all sorts of mischief.

If you look at the hand carefully, you can see how like your own it is, with four fingers and a thumb. If you could hold this hand in yours, you would feel its softness and know how like your own the touch of it is. The fingertips are made to feel things with, the fingernails to protect them. The thumb helps the fingers pick things up and carry them near the eyes so they can be studied closely. The owner of this grasping hand has sharp eyes and a clever brain. His mind is full of curiosity, and he uses his hands and eyes to help him satisfy his need to find out about the world around him.

Of course in some ways his hand is different from yours.

It is longer and narrower, with the curved shape of a hook. The thumb is farther away from the fingers, branching out near the wrist. The hair is thick and woolly, while on your own hand the hair is so short and fine you may need a magnifying glass to see it at all.

Nevertheless, this hand, like yours, is free to do many more things than fins, flippers, hoofs, or paws with claws can do. It can pick things up and put them down; it can push, pull, catch, open, close, and separate one thing from another. It is always reaching out for something. From the beginning, hands have helped their owners get on in the world.

The owner of this useful hand is a young, silvery-gray gibbon. Gibbons are a kind of ape. This one's name is Seymour, and his world happens to be the Education Department of the American Society for the Prevention of Cruelty to Animals in New York City.

In its red brick building with two proud, bronze horses at the gate, the ASPCA, as it is called for short, is ready to care for any animal that needs help, from a baby mouse to a tired, old horse. The ASPCA runs a hospital as well as an adoption service for unwanted animals, and children come to the Education Department from all over the city to learn about animals. If the children become Junior Members, they can help take care of those animals that live in the Education Department, either because they have been placed there for adoption or because they have been found on a street corner, abandoned by their owners. The ASPCA has a program for operating on cats and dogs so they cannot have kittens and puppies.

When morning comes, Seymour, like the other animals in the Education Department, is hungry for breakfast. It is for food his hand is reaching. He eats everything—meat, fruit, or vegetables. He loves to nibble mealworms and has to be stopped from eating too many, like a greedy person with peanuts. Only monkeys, apes, and men stuff themselves. Other animals, living in the wild, know when to stop. Carefully, Seymour picks over his food to find the tastiest morsels and even peels the skin

from grapes. He drinks with his hand, dipping it into his water dish and then licking it dry. All gibbons drink this way.

After breakfast, Red and Chris come to get Seymour from his cage. They are Junior Members who work here and know him. Seymour flips three backward somersaults to say hello to them and to show them what a clever fellow he is. His hands could easily open the fastener on his cage, so it must have a special lock and chain to keep him out of harm's way. The moment Red unlocks the door, he is out in one bound and has his arms wrapped around her neck. Sometimes when she holds Seymour—or he holds her—she feels as if he had two pairs of hands. His feet, unlike yours, can grasp too. In fact, the space between his big toe and his other toes lets him grip things with his feet even better than he can with his hooklike hands.

Whenever Seymour is being cared for by Junior Members, a grownup ASPCA staff member is always nearby. Though he is only about four years old and has always been gentle with everyone, gibbons as they grow older can sometimes be very rough.

Together Seymour, Red, and Chris walk down the hall. That is, Red and Chris walk. Seymour strides, hops, runs, and then climbs a door to swing from the top. Every trip he makes is an adventure and an exploration. He is so quick and daring that he has to wear a leash around his waist, but he holds it firmly in one hand to keep it from pulling.

Though he is a strong athlete, the gibbon, whose home is Southeast Asia and the East Indies, is much smaller than the other kinds of ape: the orangutans, also from Asia, and the chimpanzees and gorillas from Africa. Seymour weighs 12 pounds and stands 3 feet tall.

People who study animals have divided them all into separate groups according to the ways their bodies are made, the ways they are alike, and the ways they are different. Gibbons, with the other apes, belong in the division of vertebrates, because they have spinal columns, or backbones, made up of little bones called vertebrae that are joined together to help support their bodies. You can feel the vertebrae of your own spinal column by running your fingertips up and down the middle of your back. Through your skin you can also feel the other bones of your skeleton, all attached to your spinal col-

umn to keep you from collapsing like a jellyfish. As with Seymour, your spinal column supports the part of the skeleton
called the skull that holds every vertebrate's three-part brain.

Gibbons also belong in the class of animals known as mammals, because they give birth to live babies they can nurse with
their own milk from breasts, or mammary glands. Other animals give birth to eggs from which the young animal later appears—if the egg has not first been eaten by one of the many
animals fond of eating eggs. A young gibbon is fed at his
mother's breasts, while you may have been fed your milk
either from breast or bottle. Baby mammals are born with a
strong need to suck.

Like other mammals, Seymour has a great deal of energy, because he is warm-blooded. This means his body, like yours, has a built-in temperature control to keep him comfortably warm in spite of weather changes. Your body temperature, for example, stays at 98.6°F. even when outdoors the temperature drops below 32°F., snow drifts through the air, and you go sledding in the park. Cold-blooded animals, like fish, frogs, and snakes, need warm water or air around their bodies to keep them at a healthy temperature. Too much heat or cold kills them, so they tend to doze in the sun in warm parts of the world or to hibernate in places where the winter months are cold. The warm-blooded mammal's life is not so limited, and he is free to get around more.

In addition, most mammals are covered with hair that grows thicker in winter and thinner in summer. No one knows why the hair on human beings has become so skimpy.

The most important feature of mammals is a brain able to work longer and harder than the one other animals have. It is bigger and better developed. Seymour's hands opening the cage door are guided by his clever brain, and the hands putting the special lock on his door are guided by a thinking mind too.

Gibbons also belong in the order of primates. The main sign of the primate is that grasping hand of his with four fingers and a thumb to wrap around whatever he wishes, with fingernails instead of claws that get in the way. The skin on each fingertip has little ridges to help grip things. These are what make fingerprints. You can see yours with a magnifying glass. Seymour often grips the top of a door, swinging to and fro for fun and exercise.

The word "primate" means "first one," and, to become "first," primates have used their hands to pull themselves up and up. On firm ground a paw or a hoof is useful, but most primates live in trees. For this they need hands to wrap around a branch and hang on for dear life even in a high wind.

Monkeys, close relatives of Seymour, are also primates with grasping hands, though in an important way they are different from apes. A monkey like Roger, the ASPCA's abandoned capuchin, is upright when he sits, but when he walks along a branch, he goes on all fours, his legs moving forward and backward the way a dog's do. The heavier ape is upright even when he is on the go, and he can stick his arms straight out from his sides and move them around in a circle as you can. His arms are specially made so he can swing by them like the pendulum of a clock. As he swings through the trees, he grasps the branch above with his hands and the branch below with his feet. This is why Seymour's feet were made like another pair of hands with a space between his big toe and the others. Your toes, though, are neatly arranged side by side without any gaps between, because they do not have to grip anything.

When an ape is down on the ground, he can stand on his hind legs and even walk this way for a short time. His knees stay slightly bent, since they do not lock into place to hold his legs straight the way yours do. Often he must lean on the knuckles of his long arms, since his hipbones were not made to support the whole weight of his heavy body. Still, an ape does have arms instead of front legs like monkeys and other four-footed animals. An ape is a two-footed animal. So are you. Only small human babies crawl on all fours, but they soon learn to use their hands to pull themselves up onto their hind legs.

Seymour, like other gibbons who are the lightest and most agile of the apes, can walk on his hind legs more easily and for a longer time than an orangutan, chimp, or gorilla can. When Seymour goes to another part of the ASPCA building, he strides up the stairs with Red and Chris, one hand hanging onto his leash and the other waving in the air. Sometimes he puts one foot in front of the other and holds his arms out at his sides in the manner of a tightrope walker with a balance pole. Your feet are springy platforms made to be walked on, but since Seymour's feet were really made for grasping, he tends to walk on their outer edges.

Walking is just what Seymour was doing when he was found three years ago. He was still a baby, about one year old. Tired, thin, and hungry, he was wandering along the Belt Parkway in Brooklyn, New York, first thing in the morning. A surprised driver reported him to the police, who drove out, picked him up, and took him where all the city's lost, unwanted animals go: the ASPCA.

Veterinarians there ordered the food he needed, because it was obvious from his condition that he had never had enough of the right things to eat, and they prescribed treatments for a skin disease. These treatments were special baths that he loved. A young ape is nearly as helpless as a human baby, and so, unlike other animals, most primates have only one baby at a time. Swinging in the trees, the mother would be unable to handle more. When he has to grow up without his mother's protection and training, an ape needs human beings who will give him almost as much care and attention as they would give a little child. When you were a baby, you were willing to lie in

12

your crib part of each day, but you couldn't be left alone too long. You had a need to touch and be touched. The tree-living baby ape's instinct is to hang onto his mother's hair at all times, so he will be near his food and not fall.

Now that he is older, Seymour, with his busy hands and curious mind, still can't be left alone out of his cage. Everything he sees around him must at once be touched, poked, pulled, chewed, pushed, lifted, dropped, opened, climbed into, dumped over, jumped on, and in every possible way studied and found out about. He sees something, leaps toward it, and grasps it almost at the same moment—faster than any other primate.

When you were little, you explored with your hands much the way Seymour does, but as you grew older, you learned to satisfy your curiosity less dangerously. How did you learn? Grownups cried out in loud, scary voices, "No. Don't touch. You'll break it. You'll hurt yourself." You learned what each of those words meant and even learned to say them yourself, but an ape, no matter how clever, can only learn to understand the tone of voice, not the words and their real meanings. Scientists are not sure why apes can't speak. The mouth and the part of the throat used in talking seem to be shaped differently in apes than in people. Some of the difficulty may lie in the brain.

The office of the Education Department at the ASPCA is crowded with objects, animals, and people for Seymour to find out about. To Diana Henley, who is in charge of the department and all the animals, he says good morning by putting his arms around her, because they are so fond of each other.

Since Seymour can only make hooting, chattering noises,

he does his real "talking" with movements of his body and expressions of his face. When he meets friends, he smiles with lips drawn back, showing his teeth and sometimes sticking out his tongue. He throws his arms and legs around the friend and perhaps clucks and squeals. An angry gibbon smacks his lips, jumps up and down, and clicks his teeth. Like other primates, Seymour has a face that shows his feelings. His eyes are almost human, and his upper lip—not divided in two parts like a dog's—moves easily. He can pout, frown, and scowl.

We also "talk" this way. We nod, shake our heads, shrug our shoulders, stamp our feet, and make sounds like "huh" and "ow." A human being's sneer is rather like the lift of a dog's upper lip when he wants to show his long canine teeth to an enemy. The shudder you sometimes feel run over your skin is a leftover of the way nervous animals, including Seymour, can fluff up their fur to make themselves look big and scary. An animal like a dog can move his ears around to catch sounds. Primate ears lie close to the head, unmoving, but the unused ear-wiggling muscles are still there. Some people can move their ears.

When Ms. Henley puts Seymour down, the Junior Members take turns holding his leash.

Seymour dips his hand into a cool cup of morning tea, while Maude, the Persian cat, watches. She has been here for years, but Grimes, the tiger-striped cat, is a newcomer. Grimes fell

from a high window, breaking her lower jaw and two legs, and though they have healed, her owner has never come to take her home. Like Seymour, she has four long canine teeth, and because of her broken jaw, the two lower ones show even when her mouth is shut. Dogs of all sizes cover the floor of the office, making shelves and desk tops more restful for cats.

Seymour moves over to the electric typewriter on another desk. It belongs to Ms. Newman who is a member of the Education Department, and she has just removed Maude from that typewriter so she can do some letters. Carla, another Junior Member, gives Seymour some peanuts. When Ms. Newman tells Carla he has had enough, he reaches out to push Ms. Newman away and pull Carla nearer. Having learned from

16

Junior Members what bottles are for, he grasps one and drinks ginger ale in an ungibbonlike way. He balances on a wastepaper basket, snacks on a new kind of candy, studies a bottle cap, and sits down to rest on a desk no one is using. His mind and body are so active, he is soon overexcited and overtired.

When he needs to rest, he asks to have his hair combed. The asking is done by his lying down on his back near a likely person—especially when that person has a comb. If he lived with another gibbon, they would take care of each other's hair with their fingers, parting it with the left hand, picking through it with the right. This is called grooming; and monkeys and apes do it with family and friends, not only to keep their hair

clean but also to show love or respect. It is comforting, like fur licking among cats or stroking among people. Though Seymour's hair is tidy, he still feels the need for grooming even without other gibbons around him.

This need is, perhaps, an instinct—a deep, unlearned need an animal tends to feel from birth onward. The instincts scientists usually agree on are: food, having and taking care of young ones, sleep, care of the body (grooming, for example), being with others of your kind, and taking action against danger in the world around you. These are what the body craves.

You don't have to see a bed to know you're sleepy or food to know you're hungry. Sometimes scientists have a hard time deciding whether something an animal does is caused by instinct or is learned from others of his species. This is especially true in Seymour's case, since no one knows if he lived with gibbons during his first year. Scientists have tried raising apes just as though they were human babies, taking them away from their mothers right after they were born. When they did certain things in the same way other apes did, these actions were known to be instinctive. They grasped their human "mother's" clothes, for example, just as they would have grasped their own mother's hair.

Though even the simplest animal can learn, instinct rules the life of a lower animal, like a fish, much more than the life of an ape. When Seymour is in a spot where instinct doesn't help, he tries to use his large primate brain to work out his problem.

Instincts, together with the kind of body an animal has, help make him act the way he does. If an animal has fins, he must swim toward food or away from danger. If he has wings, he flies. Your feet and legs were made for walking, and if you suddenly found yourself perched high on a cliff in an eagle's nest, you would be helpless. Seymour's long arms are for reaching and swinging, and he goes on doing so even though he is in a building, not a tree. The shape of an animal's body, together with his instincts, were developed to help him live his own kind of life successfully in his own natural home. Living successfully means finding food, escaping enemies, and having young. Walking gets you where you want to go. Grooming keeps Seymour's hair free of disease-carrying insects. Seymour's instincts have not changed, any more than his body has, simply because he has been put into a new home where there are no insects.

No one knows where Seymour came from, but he may well have been brought into America illegally from Southeast Asia before being left alone on the Belt Parkway. Hunters often kill a mother ape in order to capture her baby and make money selling him to an animal dealer in another part of the world. Needless to say, most of these motherless apes die before ever reaching new homes. Some countries are passing laws to try to protect their animals against such treatment. Perhaps Seymour was one of the many pets that are dumped somewhere, anywhere, because their owners find them too much trouble. These abandoned pets may be wild animals, like ocelots, raccoons, and apes, that were designed by nature only for a free life in the wild and don't belong in houses and apartments, and in some places it is now illegal to have them there. Or they may be the usual domestic animals, like cats, dogs, and hamsters, that need food, water, medicine, time, love, and a lot more fuss than the owner had planned on.

If Seymour was born in the wild woods, it might have been among the tall trees of Thailand. His hooklike hands and the great length of his arms in proportion to his body allow him to live safely in trees. Your arms only reach partway down your thighs, while Seymour's touch the ground. His hands were made for hooking over branches and his arms for swinging from tree to tree as far as 50 feet apart. His scientific name is *Hylobates,* or "Walking on the Trees." Gibbons are known as the acrobats of the animal kingdom. They are more graceful in the branches of their leafy homes than circus performers among their tra-pezes. And they can "tightrope" walk on long vines.

Among ground-dwelling animals males tend to be larger than females, but among tree-dwellers like Seymour sex causes little difference in size.

Gibbons, some of which are black, tan, gray, or silvery white, live in family groups—father, mother, one or two youngsters, and sometimes a very old gibbon, perhaps a grand-father or mother. Among the four kinds of apes, only gibbons enjoy this close way of living rather like your own. The family wakes at dawn after a night together in their sleeping tree, because, also like us, the higher primates sleep at night and are up and about during the day. Gibbons are the only apes that do not build nests but sleep curled up in a ball of fur, so the rain can run off, or else stretched out full length on a branch. They have rough pads on their bottoms to make branch sitting less uncomfortable. For an hour or more after waking, they greet the dawn and their neighbors with cries that have been called songs and set down on paper like music. Each family claims as its own a certain amount of land, or rather the trees on that land, and their morning songs may be a way of letting other gibbon families know these particular trees are lived in. The songs may also be just for the fun of it, the way some ASPCA Junior Members sing in the shower of a morning.

After the morning concert, the family spends the rest of the day, except for a midday nap, traveling through its trees, eating the fruits, leaves, and even flowers found along the way. Seymour's long canine teeth are needed for tearing the rinds of fruits. Your canines are short. Gibbons also like to nibble on insects, eggs, and birds. A gibbon is so swift he can catch a bird in one hand while he and it are both flying in midair.

If they find another family feasting in one of their own trees, the gibbons drive the trespassers out with threatening gestures, angry faces, and ear-splitting shouts, in a kind of gibbon king-of-the-castle game. The trespassers threaten and shout right back, of course, but in the end they retreat to their own land, where their shouts become louder, because they feel sure of themselves again. For many animals home means comfort, security, and a place to raise their young. They fight to defend these homes, but often this fighting is only a threatening show. Gibbons and other apes studied in the wild seem to be quite peaceful animals, able to settle their arguments with noise rather than bloodshed.

During the family's daily travels, the baby holds tight around his mother's body. For his first six months she bends her knees and draws up her legs to give him a safe, warm seat while she moves through the branches. Sometimes the father holds the baby, grooming or playing with him. While his parents rest, he plays follow-the-leader and tag with his brothers and sisters.

After a young ape has grown up, at the age of eight or nine, the parents drive him or her out of the family group and out of their part of the forest. This is not done suddenly. Little by little the parents make it clear to the young male or female gibbon that the time has come for it to find a mate and start a family in another place, where he or she may live to be thirty or forty years old.

Like a human child, a young gibbon lives with his parents,

protected by them and learning from them. That is the whole reason for the long childhood of primates. The minute a gibbon is born, he begins to learn from his mother and father that he is a gibbon and what it is gibbons do and don't do. As he grows older, his parents help him learn to move safely along the family's path through the trees high above the ground, for in spite of being athletes with the best eyesight of any primate, gibbons do fall. Their only enemies are leopards, pythons, and men. Among animals in the wild, half the young are lost through sickness and accidents. Only man with his medicines and hospitals can save almost all his babies.

But Seymour will never know the beauty or the danger of the life of a free gibbon. Seymour, instead, is a working gibbon, one of the many apes and monkeys used in zoos and laboratories around the world for the study of primates.

The job for Seymour and the other animals in the Education Department is helping children learn about animals, either at the ASPCA itself or in schools and day camps around the city. When the animals travel, everybody piles into a small bus called the Arkmobile. Seymour enjoys the ride through the city streets, climbing about in the back and peering out of the windows. At the end of the trip he investigates the bus thoroughly, inside and out, with Michael, a Junior Member, holding onto his leash.

Before showing the animals to the children in a day camp the Arkmobile is visiting, one of the staff members tells them about the ASPCA and how it was started in 1866 in New York City by Henry Bergh, a man who felt that he must stop people from beating horses, putting on dog- and cockfights, or being in

any way cruel to animals. He said, "Men will be just to men when they are kind to animals." His ideas were made fun of, because at that time people thought animals different from human beings and far beneath them in every way.

But if you look closely, you can see that, though at first glance animals may seem very different from us, there are more likenesses than differences. When the staff member shows Seymour to the children, they gather around to feel his fur with their hands while he reaches out to touch them with his.

Seymour and all the other vertebrates share the same general body plan—skeleton, brain, blood moving through all parts of the body—and always have ever since they began to appear on the earth long, long ago. Seymour's body, like every other animal's, has been made so he can do the two most important things: get food and save himself from danger. An animal's life in the water, on the ground, in the air, or in trees makes demands on him that he must meet or die. It is possible, however, for small changes to take place ever so slowly in the bodies of certain animals. These changes are brought about by changes in the genes, those particles in each cell in your body that control what comes to you from your parents and what you pass on to your children. Sometimes a generation is skipped. You have red hair and long legs, and so did your grandmother.

If these changes mean that these animals can do a better job of living, they are successes. Their chances for successful changes are passed on by way of the genes to their many offspring. There begin to be more and more of these animals doing a better job of living, all passing on their genes in turn, and as a rule one helpful change leads to another. On the other hand, the animal whose body fails to fit him for life in his world dies before he can have young, causing his kind to disappear altogether. A weak gibbon falls from a tree before he has a mate and babies. The sign that a species of animal is an evolutionary success is that there are lots of them.

When enough changes have taken place in the bodies of certain successful animals and a new home and way of life turn up, a new kind of animal appears. For example, long ago when the waters of the world began to dry up, certain fish with four fins that were like stumpy lobes used these fins to push themselves over the ground toward the water pools that were left. Inside each fin were bony stiffeners—the beginning skeleton of a leg and five-part paw. In the process, they had to learn to breathe air with lungs they had probably started developing even before they left water, and to find new foods, perhaps good-to-eat worms they'd never tasted before. Of course this didn't happen because those fish were trying to become another kind of animal. On the contrary, they were only trying to go on being good fish, but the change happened because of the demands put upon them by earth and air. Another example is an animal that in the distant past developed wings so it could take to the air, where insects were plentiful, and could follow this food supply. In this way, amphibians—the crawlers through pools—and birds, like the parrot being shown to the children at the day camp, came into existence.

The right animal in the right place at the right time is able by chance to move on to new ways of living, but it is the forces outside not inside the body that cause change, like the change from fin to paw to Seymour's grasping hand.

These changes take huge stretches of time to happen. Trying to imagine the time needed to create all the vertebrates there are in the world today, in addition to all the ones that have died out, is like looking at a star in the night sky and trying to imagine how many miles away it is.

This slow change in animals, and plants too, through many generations is called evolution. Since each kind of animal has developed from another, passing on by way of its genes chances for more change, each shows the same sort of body. One of the signs of evolution is all the likenesses in the general body plan common to vertebrates, mammals, and primates. Evolution, though, never goes in a straight line. It zigs and zags and even goes around in circles, as in the case of mammals, like dolphins, that probably went back to living in the sea after a period on land.

Seymour shares with the other animals from the ASPCA, which a staff member shows to day campers, the advantages of being a vertebrate. The fish (the first vertebrate in the world), the frog (an amphibian), the boa constrictor and turtle (both reptiles), the parrot (a bird), the cat and the dog (mammals), all have the same kind of skeleton under their skins to hold up their bodies and a skull to cover and protect the brain.

Except for the apes, like Seymour, these are all animals with tails. Seymour, and the other apes of today, have none. Or has he? The vertebrae for Seymour's tail lie down at the end of his backbone, buried away under his skin. You have those same little hidden bones too and even a set of unused muscles to move them with.

Except for the fish, these animals from the ASPCA have necks of different lengths that are useful in looking for food or enemies. Seymour turns his head on his neck quickly to see first this way, then that. So do giraffes, and so do you. Almost all mammal necks, no matter how long, have the same number of vertebrae in them—seven. These are also animals with bony jaws. Without them, how would Seymour and you chew your food?

Most vertebrates have two pairs of legs, or limbs, all because the first fish in ancient seas happened to have four fins. Most important, though, were the five stiffeners inside the fins of the first land-crawling fish. Only because there happened to be five stiffeners does Seymour have five fingers on each hand and five toes on each foot.

All vertebrates, including Seymour, need the oxygen they get from either water or air to keep their bodies going. The

oxygen travels through the body in the blood, where some salt is also found—a leftover bit of a long-ago ocean.

Both the fish and Seymour—and the other vertebrates—have the three-part vertebrate brain, though Seymour's is much larger than the fish's. The mammal's nose, eyes, and ears, all controlled by his brain, tell him more about the world around him than the fish, amphibian, or reptile can ever know. He has a four-part heart sending more blood to his brain and other parts of his body, so they all are able to do a better job.

As a mammal, Seymour's world is wider than that of other vertebrates due to his warm-bloodedness. Because it is possible for him to be always up and about, no matter what the temperature, his brain grew larger in the process of evolution, and his senses, too, were sharpened.

Before birth, a young mammal, like Seymour, is carried about inside his mother's body, kept warm, protected from enemies, and nourished through her blood stream until he is big enough to be born. Afterward his mother feeds him milk and later teaches him how to find his own food. She is always ready to help and defend him. Like other mammals, a gibbon uses his brain and his senses in caring for his young.

Fish, amphibians, and reptiles lay eggs—many more of them than will ever be hatched or grow up, because eggs in water or on land are always in danger of being eaten or otherwise destroyed. The size of the animal growing inside is limited by the size of the egg and the amount of food stored in it.

Since their young are given so much care, mammals don't need to have as many young ones as fish, amphibians, or reptiles. Even though some babies will be lost, enough will live to grow up and have young of their own. In the case of primates like Seymour, where there is only one baby and even the father helps to care for it, the young really get off to a good start in life. Although you like to be by yourself sometimes, as long as you are young, you need grownups for lots of things.

Of great importance to mammals in all their doings is their well-developed skeleton. With strong, flexible legs they can go almost anywhere and do almost anything. They run, burrow, glide, swim, hop, climb, fly, or swing—their energy and curiosity take them all over their world. By learning to move in these different ways, many mammals' limbs have been changed. Whales, for example, have lost their paws and legs. The dog stands on the tips of his four toes, having lost one on each paw. A horse has lost all but one of his toes and has strengthened it with a hoof. In the bat the front legs have turned into wings. Basically, though, the skeleton remains the same, and most mammals still have to depend on all four legs for getting around.

There was, though, a long-ago mammal that climbed up into the trees and became a primate. He felt safer out of reach of enemies, perhaps, and with so many leaves and fruits to eat he could stay there and not come down. He probably had the curiosity and the need to explore that all primates have. Seymour, of course, tries to let nothing stand in the way of his curiosity. He always climbs up and looks about in any tree he can get to.

The earliest tree climber only had paws, but in trying to hang onto his branch, the digits of his front and back paws divided, so in time they were able to grasp things the way Seymour does. Hanging on by wrapping fingers and toes

around branches was safer than digging in with claws. The tree climber began to have fingernails and toenails instead, and his fingertips became soft and able to feel everything.

As this little primate spent his time climbing up, hand over hand, the weight of his body fell on his hind legs. They developed into strong supports, and his arms and grasping hands were free to reach out to find out about things in this leafy new world with the help of his eyes.

Animals living on the ground, like the ASPCA's beagle

Amy, find out about things with their moist, whiskery noses. You can hardly imagine how much Amy is able to learn about her world with her nose, because like Seymour you use your eyes and hands so much more than your nose. Think of having to catch, fix, and eat your meals without hands. For an animal, like a boa constrictor, going about on the ground, the nose is most important, so it's right up front, while his eyes are on the sides of his head so he can see without turning. He sees two pictures at a time, and everything looks flat.

The long-ago primate, awake in the daytime up in the trees, stopped using his nose for tracking. The branch he climbed had fewer smells to sniff, but more things to look at. His whole sense of touch moved from whiskery nose to soft fingers. He sat down in his tree, held his head up, studied a piece of fruit with his eyes by the light of day, and popped it into his mouth with

his fingers. You can find out more about your food by looking at it than by sniffing at it.

It was not only for food the primate needed sharp eyes. If Seymour lived in a forest, flying from tree to tree, and did not see clearly, he would fall. Seymour's primate eyes are set close together in the front of his head and see only one picture at a time, as yours do. This picture shows him how far it is from where he is to somewhere else. That is, it shows him depth.

While the primate's eyes and fingers became more important, his muzzle got smaller, and he lost his damp nose and whiskers altogether. As the part of the primate's brain that told his nose what to do became less important, the part in charge of his eyes, hands, and feet grew. His knowing how to take hold of anything he wanted, to feel it with his fingers, and to study it with his eyes, made that part of his brain grow larger. He began to be better able to remember the past, to think about what is going on right now, and maybe even to plan for the future.

This primate way of life in trees led from monkeys to apes, from standing flat on four feet to almost balancing on two. Mixing up the two kinds of animals, however, is as wrong as mixing up monkeys and men. The ape not only has more useful arms but also hipbones made to carry more weight. When a four-footed animal stands on his hind legs, his insides slide downward, but Seymour's insides are held in place. The upper part of his body is shorter and wider than a monkey's. No apes have tails, but many monkeys do. Roger can use his like a fifth hand.

Most of the long-ago apes—ancestors of today's gibbons,

orangutans, chimpanzees, and gorillas—grew used to staying in warm forests where life was easy. There was, though, another kind of ape who came down out of the trees to live on the ground, perhaps in Africa. He is thought to have been about four feet tall and hairy. His ears looked like yours, and he did a great deal of noisy calling as gibbons do. He may have had a tail as early gibbons did. Possibly he had been swinging from branch to branch long enough to have the two-footed walk of an ape but not long enough to develop Seymour's long arms and hooklike hands. No one knows why he left the safety of his old home for the dangers of open, flat land where he had to face all the hunting animals. Perhaps his curiosity and the wish to try new foods got the better of his fears. Perhaps just as the first land-living fish were looking for new pools, this primate was only trying to reach trees too far away for jumping.

Whatever the reason for his starting a new life, it caused changes in his body. Almost from the start his teeth were different from any ape's. His front ones including the canines were smaller, possibly because of eating different foods than apes. One of the most important changes was his learning to walk altogether upright on two feet without any help from his hands, though at first he was probably better at running than walking. When his hind legs and hipbones were able to carry the weight of his body, he could look out over the countryside. His hands began to be completely free. The two things went together really—balancing on the springy hind feet and freeing the hands.

As soon as this new animal's hands no longer had to hold up his body, they began to do all sorts of things. They became very movable, with the thumb meeting the fingertips. He moved his hands around with ease because he had two bones in his forearm that came to him from two tiny bones in the fins of the first land-crawling fish. Right away he might have learned to carry his food in his hands. Next this new ape, who had no claws, long canine teeth, or horns, may have decided to pick up rocks, sticks, and bones to use for tools and weapons. He couldn't fight like the animals that had fangs and claws, nor could he run like the animals that had hoofs.

The more the new ape thought about it, the more he found for his hands to do. And the more his hands did, the more his primate brain grew.

This animal was rather strange looking. His head had a lot of room for brains and a pushed-in face with a bony, pointed nose and chin sticking out. He had less hair than most mammals, most of it on top in a bush. His spine had an s-curve, and he had long, muscular legs, and buttocks to sit on. No longer did he have to sit in a tree in a warm forest, for every part of the world was open to him. He could cross rivers and mountains. His two hind feet had to carry a heavy load as he walked and sometimes they got tired.

This new vertebrate-mammal-primate became man, the hunter, with a body not too different from those of all his living relatives, especially his close cousins, the apes. Not only does his body show he is related, but so do many of his actions. Evolution has formed and worked on animal behavior just as it has on bodies.

All young animals, especially mammals, like to play. Human beings have probably played hide-and-seek since the first children appeared on earth. Leapfrog, tag, tug-of-war, and coasting are also well loved by different kinds of animals. Games are ways of reaching out with mind and paws or hands to find out about the world. Besides they are fun.

After resting during the trip home from the day camp in the Arkmobile, Seymour wants to play. In a cupboard in the office of the Education Department he often finds Marmalade, a golden cat, the only animal willing to play with him. The other animals like to play, but not with Seymour. Marmalade, though, is always ready for a game of hide-and-seek. They dodge in and out of the cupboards, watched by Maximilian T. Fang, an old dog, whose blanket Seymour has dragged into the game. Max has lost all his fur as a result of a skin disease, and he enjoys a blanket. Chris returns it to him. Then Seymour pushes open another cupboard door, and Marmalade has a new hiding place.

What then is the great difference that sets Chris, Red, Carla, Michael, and you so apart from Seymour and the big apes?

Could it be your primate brain—not different in structure from theirs, but bigger, able to learn more and to work out really hard problems—telling your primate hand what to do that makes you more powerful than Seymour and all the other animals in the world?

A chimpanzee can make and use small tools, but he can get along quite well without any, while you would have a hard time indeed if you had to do without a single one of the many things man has made. Seymour can understand that by pushing Ms. Newman away and pulling Carla closer, he can get more nuts right away, but your mind can look ahead to tomorrow and

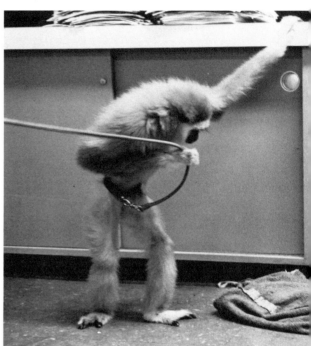

many tomorrows to come. A gibbon can sing his songs, but you can think in words and can even write down your thoughts so other people perhaps hundreds of years later can read them and learn from them. Man is the language animal.

Only you can use your hands and mind to find out about primates, so you can learn from today's monkeys and apes something of what your own forgotten beginnings were like. For years scientists have studied animals in laboratories and zoos, but now they have begun to work with them in their own natural homes. They have decided an animal will only show his real self and way of living when he is free in the wild. Life in a laboratory shows him in a different light, using his intelligence to solve other kinds of problems. Dr. George B. Schaller, with a notebook instead of a gun, followed family groups of gorillas on their wanderings in search of food through their African homeland. Dr. Jane van Lawick-Goodall went to live in Africa with a troop of chimpanzees, using carefully protected boxes of bananas as bait. One of the first of these patient watchers in the wild, Dr. Clarence Carpenter, sat for months on a cliff in Thailand so he could tell us about the home life of gibbons. These scientists have all written about what they've done so others can learn.

Oddly enough, scientists believe men began to fight with and destroy nature almost from the start. Certain mammals began to disappear at the same time early man learned to use hand axes and fire. Putting to the torch many acres of land to flush out game killed many more animals than a small tribe could possibly eat.

Today, with ever more men on earth each day, many animals are losing their homes even faster because of what men are doing with their clever brains and strong hands, for man is the only animal who can change the world. With his tools and weapons, man destroys animals. They are exterminated not only by shooting and trapping, but also by chopping down trees and paving fields where they once found their food and made homes. Other animals can find nothing to eat after man has used his poisons to get rid of the insects and animals he has decided he doesn't like. Whenever man changes the world, he changes evolution, and evolution is going on right now for us all—fish, apes, and men. Now, though, what was once controlled only by the forces of nature is also run by the hand of man.

The worst problem comes when man has to choose, as he must in Africa and Asia, between land for himself and land for the stalking tiger and many other vanishing animals. Love of animals comes more easily to men who are not hungry.

The only answer to these problems lies with you. Just as you are the only animal who can change the world, you are the only animal who can work to save all the others.

When Seymour holds out his hand to Carla as they walk down the hall at the ASPCA, he is showing in the only way he can the trust so many animals must put in man if we are all to go on living together.

PART TWO

W̲ould you like to start watching, studying, and helping animals? You can begin today no matter where you live.

Following is a partial list of different kinds of organizations in the United States that are working to help animals here and abroad. You can add to the list, either by finding other groups or starting your own branch of a national organization. This may give you ideas about what to look for near home or when you are on vacation. Not only is the list incomplete, it is also subject to change, because people move, or space is lacking, or money runs low. Some programs are for nursery-school children, others for high-school students, some for all ages. Some cost money, while others are free. If you show you really care and are ready to work hard, the time may come when a museum or center that doesn't at first seem to have room for you will suddenly find something you can do to help.

One of the first places to look for animals is in a zoo or aquarium. Perhaps you're lucky enough to live near one like the Miller Park Zoo in Bloomington, Illinois, where they have many workshops for their Junior Zoo Keepers, who work with the animals side by side with grown-up zoo keepers. Perhaps you live near a small one like the Sunset Zoo in Manhattan, Kansas, where everyone in town helps out. The veterinarian who runs this zoo began it in 1933 as a hobby. The St. Louis Zoo is known around the world, and over in Honolulu, the Waikiki Aquarium has a shell club for young people who swap shells. No reptiles, amphibians, or land mammals, except one species of bat, are native to Hawaii.

Until recently, zoological gardens, as they are sometimes called, were usually thought of as places for entertainment not education. The earliest zoos were for the private amusement of kings and queens, but the people of the town were sometimes expected to provide the animals' food. The poor person found it hard to understand why a king's pets should have enough to eat and warm homes when his own people did not. Later on, when zoos were for everyone's use, people went there to picnic and laugh at the strange animals begging for food.

Now, zoo people are hard at work behind the scenes trying to keep alive the species of animals that are losing their natural homes, for they are so few in numbers they face sure extinction. Since the 1600s, man has helped to bring about the extinction of approximately 200 different kinds of mammals alone. About 42 species of birds have vanished from the world in the last 280 years.

Often a zoo finds it hard enough to find a pair of rare animals, harder still to keep them alive, and sometimes impossible to breed. Unless an animal feels at home in captivity with its mate, it will never have young. The International Union for Conservation of Nature and Natural Resources keeps lists, as does the Office of Endangered Species of the United States Department of the Interior, of the animals in greatest danger, and zoo people—by selling, trading, or lending among themselves —try to make sure these animals will live on. About twice as many Siberian tigers live in zoos as in the wild, and since those that are free number only 100 to 150, it is felt that in another ten years they will be gone. On the other hand, such once nearly extinct animals as the American bison, Père David's deer, the Arabian oryx, the wild cattle of Chillingham, the wisent or European bison, and the nene or Hawaiian goose have been brought back by being carefully rescued and bred in captivity. The same can be said of Przewalski's horse, an animal that looks like the ones seen in the ancient cave paintings. Some of these animals are now being returned to their homes in the wild.

Sadly, in years to come, with the world's forests growing smaller, water growing dirtier, and human population growing larger, many more animals will be making their last stand in zoos and aquariums. You might want to help them by learning to take part in this work.

Remember as you watch zoo animals, however, that their behavior is different from the way it would be in the wild where they are busy every minute hunting for food or defending themselves. Maybe the "zoo" of the future will be a place where animals, though protected from people, will have enough space to roam relatively freely in natural surroundings with hiding places. Jim Fowler's Animal Forest in South Carolina is like this. Only animals that are or were, long ago, native to the area are kept there on land and in a climate that suits them.

Another place to learn about wildlife is a museum of natural history or science. Some of them are for young people only. Brooklyn's Children's Museum, the oldest one in the world, is known to neighborhood youngsters as their MUSE. The Alexander Lindsay Junior Museum in Walnut Creek, California, offers a junior-aide program and an animal lending library. Little Rock, Arkansas, has its Museum of Science and Natural History where high-school students serve as junior curators, helping run a regular museum for grownups. Ask your nearest museum for programs for your age group.

Many people feel strongly that no animal should ever be kept in a cage. Your pet cat, a domestic animal, has the run of your house, and he can hide in a closet if he feels the need, while in some zoos the tiger, a wild animal, is caged in a space too small for him, with nowhere to go to get away from the eyes of all the people watching him. Every animal must have a place where he can hide.

For people who don't like zoos, the right places for animal watching are nature or conservation centers, wildlife refuges or sanctuaries, and parks. Although in these areas animals are often fed in winter, cared for when they are sick or injured, and perhaps even kept caged a short time for study, they are generally free to come and go and their behavior is more natural. To see wildlife in the wild you can't sit in your car. Remembering how animals try to fit into their backgrounds, you must learn to act like an Indian—with camera and binoculars if possible. Get up as early as the day-waking animals do; wear something of a neutral color, like brown, gray, or green; stick to the trails, walking softly, stepping first on your toes and then on your heels. Most of all, learn to use your senses. Keep your eyes open for moving grass. Listen for small rustlings. With your fingertips, feel the tree bark. Even try sniffing the air. Be patient—it's worth it. And remember, as the Pleasant Valley Sanctuary of Lenox, Massachusetts, puts it: "Take only pictures. Leave only footprints."

On the other hand, in places where bears and other dangerous animals live, you do not want to melt silently into the landscape. You must let them know where you are by the noises you make, or you may risk bumping into them.

In the Jamaica Bay Wildlife Refuge, where the air is full of New York City's soot and the vapor trails from Kennedy International Airport jets, you can watch snowy egrets fishing or a mother bird pretending her wing is broken. Scientists call this "broken wing decoy behavior." The bird is torn between two instincts: to save herself by flying away or to save her young by staying with them. Unable to decide, she runs in circles dragging a wing. You might even see a lone bald eagle, the bird that is on the United States coat-of-arms but is also on The International Union for Conservation of Nature and Natural Resources' list of animals in danger of disappearing. Parts of the refuge have been planted with trees and bushes full of the seeds, berries, and nuts birds like most.

As people become more and more worried about the loss of

green spaces for animals to live in, more and more nature and conservation centers are sprouting. Woldumar Nature Center, a National Environmental Education Landmark, in Lansing, Michigan, offers Camp Discovery, nature walks over pine-needle trails, and a "sense laboratory" where the blind can touch, smell, taste, and hear the outdoors. White-tailed deer are among the most popular animals at Woldumar. On the other hand, The Plains Conservation Center near Denver, Colorado, is dry prairie with trails on which, if you look carefully, you may see antelope, prairie dogs, and perhaps even a coyote. Only the rattlesnake is not invited. Here, as in other centers, work is going on to bring the land to life again, as nearly as possible as it was before the days of supermarkets and superhighways. Students help out in programs at the Conservation Center for Creative Learning in Lander, Wyoming.

Some refuges are set up for special kinds of animals. America's last wild horses are the descendants of the horses brought over from Spain by the conquistadors. They later ran wild and became famous as Indian mounts. Wild burros, descendants of Northeast Africa's wild ass, were also brought to America by the Spaniards and later used as pack animals by western miners. The International Society for the Protection of Mustangs and Burros and WHOA! of Reno, Nevada are both led by "Wild Horse Annie" Johnston, who has been fighting for these animals for years. In December, 1971, when the President of the United States signed into law a measure protecting them on public lands, he remarked that Congress had been stormed by mail from children demanding passage of the law.

Write to The Committee for the Preservation of the Tule

Elk in Los Angeles, California, and they will tell you how you can help this rare animal. When white men reached the coast of America, they found at least six kinds of elk, properly known as *wapiti*. The eastern type was hunted to death almost immediately, leaving us only one skin and a few skulls to remind us of its beauty. The Merriam elk of Arizona and New Mexico is gone now, too. Only the Rocky Mountain elk is holding its own. The few remaining Tule or dwarf valley elk have won a small corner of California, but hunting is still sometimes allowed.

The Beaver Defenders, whose motto is "They shall never be trapped anymore," run the Unexpected Wildlife Refuge, Inc., in Newfield, New Jersey, and send out a monthly newsletter with suggestions for protecting other animals as well as beavers.

Birds of prey have a sanctuary on Hawk Mountain in Pennsylvania, while the Audubon Society, named for the American naturalist and artist, John James Audubon, has branches all over the country that try to protect and keep track of birds. The Massachusetts Audubon Society is especially busy with forty-three sanctuaries. Some Audubon members on the West Coast had to sit up nights trying to guard one lone family of peregrine falcons from thieves who crept up the rocks to the nest under cover of darkness. These endangered birds easily fall prey, when they are young, to people who fancy themselves as falconers. They wish to train the birds to hunt for them as royalty did in the Dark Ages but often end by killing them instead.

Your local university or college biology or zoology departments are places you can call for information on animal programs. Michigan State University runs the W. K. Kellogg Bird Sanctuary in Augusta with workshops, camping, and hiking.

During a California drought, starving animals came down out of the hills into the town of Sierra Madre. The Director of Parks and Recreation decided they should stay there, and now the whole town has become a wildlife refuge, where trapping, killing, and the using of residual pesticides are outlawed.

If the area where you live has no such riches to offer you, perhaps it does have a park. New York City, where people live elbow to elbow, has nine wilderness and natural areas in its parks, with nature trails and nature study programs. Just let somebody try to touch one of New York's parks, and the citizens swarm out like hornets. In Indianapolis, Indiana, where youngsters also have their own Children's Museum, the Park Department gives nature walks. So does Otter Creek Park in Vine Grove, Kentucky, and many other places. Call your Park and Recreation Department, and if it has no program—write the mayor.

Perhaps your county, like the Hamilton County Park District in Ohio, has parks with nature activities for the whole family. Also remember to write to your state capital about its parks. Delaware has the Trap Pond State Park with an island trail, the Cape Henlopen State Park with pinelands and seaside trails, and the Brandywine State Park with workshops, an explorers' club, a summer day camp, and a junior naturalist program. You may not live near any state parks but keep them in mind when traveling. If you write before you go, the park superintendent will often send you maps of trails and booklets describing the animals and plants to be seen.

Throughout the country a growing number of schools use parks and nature centers as outdoor classrooms. Everyone in certain grades has the chance to spend a day or a week on a field trip or a camp-out. Nature is no longer only a word in a book but something to see, touch, smell, and hear. The Supplementary Educational Center in Salisbury, North Carolina, even runs its own small zoo. At the Woodstock Country School in Vermont there are two bird-banding stations, the only ones in the United States run solely by high-school students.

In 1903, President Theodore Roosevelt started the first United States National Wildlife Refuge to protect the nests of pelicans and herons. It is Pelican Island, on the east coast of Florida. He later opened others.

The United States Department of the Interior, Fish and Wildlife Service, Washington, D.C. 20240, will send you a map showing all the wildlife refuges it runs today, and there are a lot of them. The department will also send you a list of the refuges where your chances for animal watching and photographing are best. It is always wise before going to the refuge to write and find out the seasons when viewing is possible.

Unlike most private sanctuaries, hunting and fishing is allowed in some federal refuges, though the dictionary says a refuge is "a place of safety," and though many of the animals seeking sanctuary are on the danger list. Lumbermen, cattlemen, and sheepherders should not be allowed to use public land. Every bit of public land belongs to you, so you can write to the government and protest this practice. There are other, better ways of cutting the animal population when a refuge becomes crowded.

Because too many people who own animals shouldn't, you will find humane societies in many cities and towns trying to save animals like Seymour, the gibbon, and Grimes, the cat. Yours may be called the Society for the Prevention of Cruelty to Animals, the Animal Rescue League, or the Anti-Cruelty Society. Look them up in your telephone book. These are the people to see when you find an animal hurt or lost—really lost, that is, not just out for a stroll, though with so many cars about pets should never be allowed to roam. Often humane societies join in animal programs with the Girl Scouts, Campfire Girls, Four-H Clubs, Boy Scouts, or Boys' Clubs of America.

Suppose, though, you live a hundred miles, as the whooping crane flies, from the nearest zoo, museum, nature center, park, or humane society. There's some wildlife around, but you've been watching it disappear long enough. Now you want to *do* something. Or perhaps your neighborhood is all paved over, and nobody seems to care—except you. You'd at least like to know how to go about planting a tree for the pigeons to roost in.

You can do any number of things.

A letter to KIND, The National Humane Education Center in Waterford, Virginia, will bring you information about their three clubs for three different age groups. They will try to put you in touch with members of the branch club nearest you, but if none exists, you can start your own, with the help of a few friends. If your whole school class signs up, you will have a class club. Or you can just join on your own. Each club picks its own name and projects to work on, and each age group gets a monthly newsletter with information about animals and suggestions on things you can do for them. The Canadian and American Wolf Defenders, whose newsletter is HOWL, works with KIND.

Two other organizations glad to help are The American Humane Association in Denver, Colorado and The Latham Foundation for the Promotion of Humane Education in Oakland, California. They each publish a magazine, sponsor TV programs, and have a Brother Buzz Junior Humane Club.

For more information about clubs and junior humane groups, no matter where you live, you can write to the Massachusetts SPCA's American Humane Education Society in Boston. The Massachusetts SPCA was founded only a year after the ASPCA and owns a nature center and a rest farm for retired horses.

Of course Ms. Diana Henley, head of the Education Department of the ASPCA in New York City, will send you information and suggestions. She has had plenty of experience with young people and animals. She would prefer, though, that you not ask how to take care of an animal after it has been hurt. For that you need to get professional help quickly.

Then there are general organizations like Cleveland Amory's The Fund for Animals, Inc. in New York City, Friends of the Earth and the Sierra Club in San Francisco, and Defenders of Wildlife in Washington, D.C. They are working hard for a world where men and animals can live together.

You might like to have a fair to raise money for the cause you decide to support. You can even, when you really know how, earn more cash by taking care of people's pets when they go on vacation, since it is both expensive and difficult to find good boarding homes for animals. And don't forget to send letters to your elected representatives and public officials, asking for passage of whatever measures you or your group are working for, urging conservation of our land and its animal inhabitants.

The possibilities are endless. Where and when you start is up to you.

*   *   *

Ferdy the ferret, a wild mammal rescued in New York
City by the Education Department of the ASPCA, gets
ready to take his bath.

Some Organizations Interested
In Animal Care and Conservation

ALABAMA

Calhoun County Humane Society
927 Zinn Dr.
Anniston, Ala. 36201

De Soto State Park
Fort Payne, Ala. 35967

Humane Education and Animal
   Control Committee
412 Syracuse St.
Mobile, Ala. 36608

Montgomery Humane Society
3599 Mobile Highway
Montgomery, Ala. 36108

Talladega National Forest
Box 35
Talladega, Ala. 35160

Tuscaloosa County Humane Society
Box 5832
Tuscaloosa, Ala. 35401

ALASKA

Tongass National Forest
Box 1628
Juneau, Alaska 99801

Mount McKinley National Park
McKinley Park, Alaska 99755

ARIZONA

Picacho Peak State Park
Box 275
Picacho, Ariz. 85241

Arizona–Sonora Desert Museum
Box 5607
Tucson, Ariz. 85703

Saguaro National Monument
Box 17210
Tucson, Ariz. 85710

Chiricahua National Monument
Dos Cabezas Star Route
Willcox, Ariz. 85643

ARKANSAS

Hot Springs National Park
Box 1219
Hot Springs, Ark. 71901

Little Rock Zoological Gardens
108 City Hall
Little Rock, Ark. 72201

Museum of Science and Natural
   History
MacArthur Park
Little Rock, Ark. 72202

CALIFORNIA

Berkeley–East Bay Humane Society
2700 9th St.
Berkeley, Calif. 94710

Friends of the Sea Otter
Big Sur, Calif. 93920

Canadian and American Wolf
   Defenders
68 Panetta Rd.
Carmel Valley, Calif. 93924

Environmental Studies Program for
   Youth
Department of Education
2314 Mariposa St.
Fresno, Calif. 93721

Fresno Audubon Society
4105 E. Farrin
Fresno, Calif. 93726

Fresno Museum of Natural History
1944 N. Winery Ave.
Fresno, Calif. 93703

Sulphur Creek Park Nature and
   Science Center
1801 D St.
Hayward, Calif. 94541

San Joaquin County Outdoor
   Education School
San Francisco YMCA Camp
Jones' Gulch
La Honda, Calif. 94020

University of California, San Diego
Scripps Aquarium–Museum
8602 La Jolla Shores Dr.
La Jolla, Calif. 92037

El Dorado Nature Center
7550 E. Spring St.
Long Beach, Calif. 90815

California Museum of Science and
   Industry
700 State Dr.
Los Angeles, Calif. 90037

Committee for the Preservation of
   the Tule Elk
5502 Markland Dr.
Los Angeles, Calif. 90022

Department of Recreation and
   Parks
Park Ranger Section
4730 Crystal Spring Dr.
Los Angeles, Calif. 90027
(Write for list of trails and
   projects.)

Los Angeles Zoo
5333 Zoo Dr.
Los Angeles, Calif. 90027

Natural History Museum
900 Exposition Blvd.
Los Angeles, Calif. 90007

Outdoor Education Office
Bellevue Youth Services Center
   Branch
3317 Bellevue Ave.
Los Angeles, Calif. 90026

East Bay Regional Park District
11500 Skyline Blvd.
Oakland, Calif. 94619

The Latham Foundation
Latham Square Bldg.
Oakland, Calif. 94612

Tucker Wildlife Sanctuary
Star Rt.
Box 858
Orange, Calif. 92667

Society for the Preservation of
   Birds of Prey
Box 293
Pacific Palisades, Calif. 90272

Pinnacles National Monument
Paicines, Calif. 95043

Living Desert Association
Box 390
Palm Desert, Calif. 92260

Jurupa Mountains Cultural Center
7621 Highway 60
Riverside, Calif. 92509

Riverside Municipal Museum
3720 Orange St.
Riverside, Calif. 92501

Department of Parks and
   Recreation
717 K St.
Sacramento, Calif. 95814

Sacramento Science Center and
   Junior Museum
4500 Y St.
Sacramento, Calif. 95817

Youth Science Center of Monterey
   County
River Rd.
Box 2095
Salinas, Calif. 93901

Junior Humane Society
887 Sherman St.
San Diego, Calif. 92110

Natural History Museum
Box 1390
San Diego, Calif. 92112

San Diego Zoo
Balboa Park
Box 551
San Diego, Calif. 92112

California Academy of Sciences
Golden Gate Park
San Francisco, Calif. 94118

Friends of the Earth
529 Commercial St.
San Francisco, Calif. 94111

The San Francisco SPCA
2500 16th St.
San Francisco, Calif. 94103

San Francisco Zoological Gardens
Zoo Rd. and Skyline Blvd.
San Francisco, Calif. 94132

Sierra Club
1050 Mills Tower
San Francisco, Calif. 94104

San Mateo County Junior Museum
Coyote Point
San Mateo, Calif. 94401

Floating Marine Laboratory
1104 Civic Center Dr. W.
Santa Ana, Calif. 92701

Child's Estate
Box 4758
Santa Barbara, Calif. 93103

Museum of Natural History
2559 Puesta del Sol Rd.
Santa Barbara, Calif. 93105

Director of Parks and Recreation
55 W. Sierra Madre Blvd.
Sierra Madre, Calif. 91024

Audubon Canyon Ranch
Shoreline Highway Rt. 1
Stinson Beach, Calif. 94970

Alexander Lindsay Junior Museum
1901 1st Ave.
Walnut Creek, Calif. 94596

Yosemite National Park
Box 577
Yosemite Village, Calif. 95389

COLORADO

Cheyenne Mt. Zoological Park
Box 158
Colorado Springs, Colo. 80901

The United Peregrine Society, Inc.
5111 Rocking R. Dr.
Colorado Springs, Colo. 80915

The American Humane Association
Box 1266
Denver, Colo. 80201

The Plains Conservation Center
9360 E. Center, Apt. 62D
Denver, Colo. 80231

Rocky Mountain National Park
Box 1080
Estes Park, Colo. 80517

Balarat Center for Environmental
  Studies
Denver Public Schools
Jamestown, Colo. 80455

CONNECTICUT

Roaring Brook Nature Center
Gracey Rd.
Box 176
Canton, Conn. 06019

Norma Terris Humane Education
  and Nature Center
East Haddam, Conn. 06423

Audubon Society, State of Conn.
2325 Burr St.
Fairfield, Conn. 06430

Audubon Center in Greenwich
613 Riversville Rd.
Greenwich, Conn. 06830

Brooksvale Recreation Park
524 Brooksvale Ave.
Hamden, Conn. 06518

Macedonia Brook State Park
Kent, Conn. 06757

The Litchfield Nature Center and
  Museum
Litchfield, Conn. 06759

Lutz Junior Museum
126 Cedar St.
Manchester, Conn. 06040

The Denison Pequotsepos Nature
  Center, Inc.
Pequotsepos Rd.
Box 42
Mystic, Conn. 06355

New Britain's Youth Museum
28 High St.
New Britain, Conn. 06051

New Canaan Nature Center
144 Oenoke Ridge
New Canaan, Conn. 06840

Peabody Museum of Natural
  History
Yale University
New Haven, Conn. 06520

Thames Science Center
Gallows Lane
New London, Conn. 06320

Sharon Audubon Center
Rt. 4
Sharon, Conn. 06069

The Norwalk Museum and Zoo
133 Lexington Ave.
South Norwalk, Conn. 06854

Stamford Museum and Nature
  Center, Inc.
39 Scofieldtown Rd.
Stamford, Conn. 06903

Mid-Fairfield County Youth
  Museum
10 Woodside Lane
Box 165
Westport, Conn. 06880

Flanders Nature Center, Inc.
Flanders Rd.
Woodbury, Conn. 06798

DELAWARE

Trap Pond State Park
Laurel, Del. 19956

Cape Henlopen State Park
Lewes, Del. 19958

Bombay Hook National Wildlife
  Refuge
R.D. 1, Box 147
Smyrna, Del. 19977

Delaware Nature Education Center
Brandywine Creek State Park
Box 3900
Wilmington, Del. 19807

DISTRICT OF COLUMBIA

Animal Welfare Institute
Box 3650
Washington, D.C. 20007

Defenders of Wildlife
2000 N St. N.W.
Washington, D.C. 20036

The Humane Society of the U.S.
1604 K St. N.W.
Washington, D.C. 20006

Rock Creek Nature Center
National Capital Parks–West
1100 Ohio Dr. S.W.
Washington, D.C. 20242

Smithsonian Institution
Washington, D.C. 20560

U.S. Department of the Interior
Fish and Wildlife Service
Washington, D.C. 20240

U.S. Department of the Interior
Office of Endangered Species
1717 H St. N.W.
Washington, D.C. 20240

U.S. Government Printing Office
Washington, D.C. 20402
(Sells booklets on National Parks
  and Forests.)

The Washington Animal Rescue
  League
71 O St. N.W.
Washington, D.C. 20001

The Wilderness Society
729 15th St. N.W.
Washington, D.C. 20005

World Wildlife Fund, Inc.
910 17th St. N.W.
Washington, D.C. 20006

FLORIDA

Hernando Audubon Society
Chinsegut Nature Center
404 Highland St.
Brooksville, Fla. 33512

Museum of Arts and Sciences
1040 Museum Blvd.
Daytona Beach, Fla. 32014

Corkscrew Swamp Sanctuary
Audubon Society
Fort Myers, Fla. 33902

The Florida State Museum
University of Florida
Museum Rd.
Gainesville, Fla. 32601

Everglades National Park
Box 279
Homestead, Fla. 33030

The Jacksonville Children's
  Museum
1025 Gulf Life Dr.
Jacksonville, Fla. 32207

The Mountain Lake Sanctuary
Lake Wales, Fla. 33853

Big Cypress Center
Rt. 3, Box 140
Naples, Fla. 33940

Central Florida Museum
810 E. Rollins Ave.
Orlando, Fla. 32803

Junior Museum of Bay County, Inc.
Box 977
Panama City, Fla. 32401

The Science Center
7701 22nd Ave. N.
St. Petersburg, Fla. 33710

J. N. "Ding" Darling National
  Wildlife Refuge
Drawer B
Sanibel, Fla. 33957

Nature's Classroom
Rt. 1, Box 396
Thonotosassa, Fla. 33592

Science Museum and Planetarium
1141 W. Lakewood Rd.
West Palm Beach, Fla. 33405

GEORGIA

Fernbank Science Center
DeKalb County Board of Education
156 Heaton Park Dr. N.E.
Atlanta, Ga. 30307

Okefenokee Science Center
Box 180
Waycross, Ga. 31501

HAWAII

Bernice P. Bishop Museum
1355 Kalihi St.
Honolulu, Hawaii 96819

Hawaii Audubon Society
Box 5032
Honolulu, Hawaii 96814

Waikiki Aquarium
2777 Kalakaua Ave.
Honolulu, Hawaii 96815

IDAHO

Department of Commerce and
  Development
Capitol Bldg.
Boise, Idaho 83707

(Write for information on parks
  and Swan Falls Bird of Prey
  Area.)

ILLINOIS

Miller Park Zoo
Parks and Recreation Department
City Hall
Bloomington, Ill. 61701

The Anti-Cruelty Society
157 W. Grand Ave.
Chicago, Ill. 60610

Lincoln Park Zoo
Chicago, Ill. 60614

Crystal Lake Outdoor Education
  Center
330 N. Main St.
Crystal Lake, Ill. 60014

Vermilion County Conservation
  District
703 Kimber St.
Danville, Ill. 61832

Beall Woods Nature Preserve
Keensburg, Ill. 62852

The Morton Arboretum
Lisle, Ill. 60532

Forest Preserve District of Cook
  County
536 N. Harlem Ave.
River Forest, Ill. 60305
(Write for list of nature centers
  and trails.)

Department of Conservation
605 State Office Building
400 S. Spring St.
Springfield, Ill. 62706
(Write for list of parks with nature
  programs.)

Lincoln Memorial Garden and
  Nature Center
2301 E. Lake Shore Dr.
Springfield, Ill. 62707

The Illinois Prairie Path
616 Delles Rd.
Wheaton, Ill. 60187

INDIANA

Children's Zoological Gardens

3411 Sherman St.
Fort Wayne, Ind. 46808

Humane Society–Calumet Area
6546 Columbia Ave.
Hammond, Ind. 46320

Children's Museum of Indianapolis
3010 N. Meridian St.
Box 88207
Indianapolis, Ind. 46208

Indianapolis Humane Society
7929 N. Michigan Rd.
Indianapolis, Ind. 46268

Indianapolis Zoological Society, Inc.
3120 E. 30th St.
Indianapolis, Ind. 46218

IOWA

Davenport Museum
1717 W. 12th St.
Davenport, Iowa 52804

Des Moines Center of Science and
  Industry
Greenwood–Ashworth Park
Des Moines, Iowa 50312

State Preserves Advisory Board
Box 424
Indianola, Iowa 50125
(Write for list.)

KANSAS

Brit Spaugh Zoological Society, Inc.
Box 215
Great Bend, Kans. 67530

Hutchinson Recreation Commission
101 S. Walnut
Hutchinson, Kans. 67501

Sunset Zoo
Manhattan, Kans. 66502

Environmental Education Project
1601 Van Buren
Topeka, Kans. 66612

Topeka Zoological Park
635 Gage Blvd.
Topeka, Kans. 66606

KENTUCKY

Bernheim Forest Nature Center
Clermont, Ky. 40110

Mammoth Cave National Park
Mammoth Cave, Ky. 42259

Union College Environmental
    Education Center
Cumberland Gap National
    Historical Park
Middlesboro, Ky. 40965

Otter Creek Park Nature Center
Rt. 1
Vine Grove, Ky. 40175

LOUISIANA

Jungle Gardens
Avery Island, La. 70513

Lafayette Natural History Museum
637 Girard Park Dr.
Lafayette, La. 70501

MAINE

Maine State Museum
State House
Augusta, Maine 04330

Mast Landing Sanctuary
Maine Audubon Society
Freeport, Maine 04032

Acadia National Park
Hulls Cove, Maine 04644

May Duff Walters Ecological
    Experimental Station
Palermo, Maine 04354

Nature Center
Maine Audubon Society
Scarborough, Maine 04074

MARYLAND

Department of Forests and Parks
State Office Building
Annapolis, Md. 21401
(Write for list of parks with trails
    and programs.)

Frederick County Outdoor School
115 E. Church St.
Frederick, Md. 21701

Greenbelt Park
Greenbelt, Md. 20770

National Capital Parks–East
5210 Indian Head Highway
Oxon Hill, Md. 20021
(Write for list of programs.)

Maryland–National Capital Park
    and Planning Commission
6000 Kenilworth Ave.
Riverdale, Md. 20840
(Write for list of nature centers.)

Maryland–National Capital Park
    and Planning Commission
8787 Georgia Ave.
Silver Spring, Md. 20907
(Write for list of nature centers.)

Montgomery County Humane
    Society
8710 Brookville Rd.
Silver Spring, Md. 20910

MASSACHUSETTS

Animal Rescue League of Boston
Tremont and Arlington Sts.

Box 265
Boston, Mass. 02117

The Children's Museum
Jamaicaway
Boston, Mass. 02130

International Society for the Protection of Animals
655 Boylston St.
Boston, Mass. 02116

Massachusetts SPCA
American Humane Education
Society
180 Longwood Ave.
Boston, Mass. 02115

Museum of Science and Hayden
Planetarium
Science Park
Boston, Mass. 02114

The Cape Cod Museum of
Natural History, Inc.
Brewster, Mass. 02631

Children's Museum, Inc.
Russells Mills Rd.
Dartmouth, Mass. 02714

Arcadia Nature Center
Easthampton, Mass. 01027

Laughing Brook Education Center
789 Main St.
Hampden, Mass. 01036

Pleasant Valley Sanctuary
Lenox, Mass. 01240

Drumlin Farm
Lincoln, Mass. 01773

Massachusetts Audubon Society
Lincoln, Mass. 01773

Stony Brook Nature Center
North St.
Norfolk, Mass. 02056

South Shore Natural Science
Center, Inc.
Jacobs Lane
Norwell, Mass. 02061

The Berkshire Museum
Pittsfield, Mass. 01201

Wachusett Meadows Sanctuary
Princeton, Mass. 01541

Moose Hill Sanctuary
300 Moose Hill St.
Sharon, Mass. 02067

Cape Cod National Seashore
South Wellfleet, Mass. 02663

Wellfleet Bay Sanctuary
Box 236
South Wellfleet, Mass. 02663

Springfield Museum of Science
236 State St.
Springfield, Mass. 01103

Trailside Museum
Forest Park
Springfield, Mass. 01108

The Elbanobscot Foundation, Inc.
Weir Hill Rd.
Sudbury, Mass. 01776

Ipswich River Sanctuary
Topsfield, Mass. 01983

Felix Neck Sanctuary
Vineyard Haven, Mass. 02568

Hale Reservation
80 Carby St.
Westwood, Mass. 02090

Worcester Science Center
222 Harrington Way
Worcester, Mass. 01604

MICHIGAN

W. K. Kellogg Bird Sanctuary

Michigan State University
12685 C Ave.
Augusta, Mich. 49012

Sarett Nature Center
Michigan Audubon Society
Benton Center Rd.
Rt. 2, Box 217
Benton Harbor, Mich. 49022

Cranbrook Institute of Science
500 Lone Pine Rd.
Bloomfield Hills, Mich. 48013

Children's Museum
67 E. Kirby
Detroit, Mich. 48202

The Huron–Clinton Metropolitan
   Authority
600 Woodward Ave.
Detroit, Mich. 48226
(Write for list of nature centers.)

The Michigan Humane Society
7401 Chrysler
Detroit, Mich. 48211

Rouge Park Nature Center
14250 W. Outer Dr.
Detroit, Mich. 48239

Drayton Plains Nature Center
2125 Denby Dr.
Box 292
Drayton Plains, Mich. 48020

Seven Ponds Nature Center
The Michigan Audubon Society
3854 Crawford Rd.
Dryden, Mich. 48428

John Ball Zoological Gardens
301 Market St. S.W.
Grand Rapids, Mich. 49502

Blandford Nature Center
1715 Hillburn Ave. N.W.
Grand Rapids, Mich. 49504

Kalamazoo Nature Center
7000 N. Westnedge Ave.
Kalamazoo, Mich. 49007

Woldumar Nature Center
5539 Lansing Rd.
Lansing, Mich. 48917

Seney National Wildlife Refuge
Seney, Mich. 49883

Fish Lake Environmental Education
   Center
Eastern Michigan University
Ypsilanti, Mich. 48197

MINNESOTA

Chippewa National Forest
Cass Lake, Minn. 56633

Hennepin County Park Reserve
   District
Rt. 1, Box 32
Maple Plain, Minn. 55359
(Write for list of nature centers.)

Wood Lake Nature Center
735 Lake Shore Dr.
Richfield, Minn. 55423

St. Paul Humane Society
Beulah Lane
St. Paul, Minn. 55108

Northwoods Audubon Center
Rt. 1
Sandstone, Minn. 55072

MISSISSIPPI

Natchez Trace Parkway
Rt. 5, NT-143
Tupelo, Miss. 38801
(Write for map and list of trails.)

MISSOURI

Jackson County Park Department

Lake Jacomo
Rt. 2, Box 408
Blue Springs, Mo. 64015

Rockwoods Reservation
Rt. 1
Glencoe, Mo. 63038

Missouri State Park Board
1204 Jefferson Building
Box 176
Jefferson City, Mo. 65101
(Write for list of parks with trails.)

Parks and Recreation Department
5600 E. Gregory
Swope Park
Kansas City, Mo. 64132

Saint Joseph Museum
11th and Charles St.
St. Joseph, Mo. 64501

The Junior Humane Society of
Missouri
1210 Macklind Ave.
St. Louis, Mo. 63110

St. Louis Zoological Park
Forest Park
St. Louis, Mo. 63110

MONTANA

Powell County Environmental
Curriculum Center
709 Missouri Ave.
Deer Lodge, Mont. 59722

Department of Fish and Game
Helena, Mont. 59601
(Educational Programs.)

Red Rock Lakes National Wildlife
Refuge
Monida Star Rt.
Lima, Mont. 59739

Bowdoin National Wildlife Refuge
Box J
Malta, Mont. 59538

Missoula County Humane Society
834 Marshall St.
Missoula, Mont. 59801

National Bison Range
Moiese, Mont. 59824

NEBRASKA

Fontenelle Forest Nature Center
1111 Bellevue Blvd. N.
Bellevue, Nebr. 68005

OSACS Science Center
316 S. County Rd.
Gretna, Nebr. 68028

Lincoln Children's Zoo
29 and A St.
Lincoln, Nebr. 68502

NEVADA

Clark County Humane Society
1621 San Pedro
Las Vegas, Nev. 89105

Valley of Fire State Park
Overton, Nev. 89040

International Society for the Protection of Mustangs and Burros
140 Greenstone Dr.
Reno, Nev. 89502

NEW HAMPSHIRE

Audubon Society of New
Hampshire
63 N. Main St.
Concord, N.H. 03301

Otter Lake Conservation School
Greenfield, N.H. 03047

Squam Lakes Science Center
Holderness, N.H. 03245

NEW JERSEY

Union County Outdoor Education
   Center
2 Glenside Park
Berkeley Heights, N.J. 07922

N.J. Audubon Society
Scherman Wildlife Sanctuary
Hardscrabble Rd.
Bernardsville, N.J. 07924

N.J. State School of Conservation
Stokes State Forest
Branchville, N.J. 07826

The Humane Society of the U.S.
N.J. Branch, Inc.
1140 E. Jersey St.
Elizabeth, N.J. 07201

Allaire State Park
Box 218
Farmingdale, N.J. 07727

The Batsto Nature House
Hammonton, N.J. 08037

Sandy Hook Environmental
   Education Center
Newman Springs Rd.
Lincroft, N.J. 07738

Morris Museum of Arts and
   Sciences
Normandy Heights and Columbia
   Rds.
Morristown, N.J. 07961

Trailside Nature and Science
   Center
Coles Ave. and New Providence
   Rd.
Mountainside, N.J. 07092

The Junior Museum of The Newark
   Museum
49 Washington St.
Newark, N.J. 07101

The Beaver Defenders
Unexpected Wildlife Refuge, Inc.
Newfield, N.J. 08344

Bergen Community Museum of Art
   and Science
Ridgewood and Farview Aves.
Paramus, N.J. 07652

Plainfield Humane Society
1401 Evergreen Ave.
Plainfield, N.J. 07060

Environmental Education Center
Lord Stirling Park
Somerset County Park Commission
Somerville, N.J. 08876

NEW MEXICO

Environmental Education
   Laboratory
Albuquerque Public Schools
724 Maple St. S.E.
Albuquerque, N. Mex. 87103

Roswell Museum
100 W. 11
Roswell, N. Mex. 88201

NEW YORK

Onondaga Nature Centers
3 Canton Street
Baldwinsville, N.Y. 13027

Bear Mountain Trailside Museums
   and Nature Trails
Administration Building
Bear Mountain, N.Y. 10911

The Heritage Museum
708 E. Tremont Ave.
Bronx, N. Y. 10457

New York Zoological Society
Bronx Park, N.Y. 10460

Brooklyn Children's Museum,
  MUSE
1530 Bedford Ave.
Brooklyn, N.Y. 11216

HAND: History, Art, and Nature
  Den, Inc.
396 South 3rd St.
Brooklyn, N.Y. 11211

N.Y. Aquarium
Boardwalk and West 8th St.
Brooklyn, N.Y. 11224

Buffalo Museum of Science
Humboldt Park
Buffalo, N.Y. 14211

Museum of the Hudson Highlands
The Boulevard
Cornwall-on-Hudson, N.Y. 12520

Ward Pound Ridge Reservation
Cross River, N.Y. 10518

Wildcliff Natural Science Center
Wildcliff Rd.
New Rochelle, N.Y. 10805

The American Museum of Natural
  History
Central Park West at 79th St.
New York, N.Y. 10024

Cleveland Amory
The Fund for Animals, Inc.
140 W. 57th St.
New York, N.Y. 10019

ASPCA
Education Department
441 E. 92nd St.
New York, N.Y. 10028

BIDE-A-WEE Home Association
410 E. 38th St.
New York, N.Y. 10016

Friends of Animals, Inc.
11 W. 60th St.
New York, N.Y. 10023

National Audubon Society
950 3rd Ave.
New York, N.Y. 10022

Parks, Recreation, and Cultural
  Affairs Administration
830 Fifth Ave.
New York, N.Y. 10021
(Write for information on parks
  with wildlife refuges.)

The Teatown Lake Reservation
Spring Valley Rd.
Ossining, N.Y. 10562

Rochester Museum and Science
  Center
657 East Ave.
Rochester, N.Y. 14607

North Shore Junior Science
  Museum
Box 223
Roslyn, N.Y. 11576

Rogers Environmental Education
  Center
Box Q
Sherburne, N.Y. 13460

Lakeside Nature Center
South Main St.
Spring Valley, N.Y. 10977

NORTH CAROLINA

Charlotte Nature Museum
1658 Sterling Rd.
Charlotte, N.C. 28209

Independence Outdoor Laboratory
1967 Patriot Dr.
Charlotte, N.C. 28212

68

Guilford County Humane Society
Box 2052
Greensboro, N.C. 27402

The Natural Science Center
4301 Lawndale Dr.
Greensboro, N.C. 27408

Department of Natural and
    Economic Resources
Box 27687
Raleigh, N.C. 27611
(Write for list of wildlife refuges.)

Supplementary Educational Center
1636 Parkview Circle
Salisbury, N.C. 28144

Weymouth Woods–Sandhills
    Nature Preserve
Box 1386
Southern Pines, N.C. 28387

NORTH DAKOTA

Dakota Zoo
Box 711
Bismarck, N. Dak. 58501

Des Lacs National Wildlife Refuge
Box 578
Kenmare, N. Dak. 58746

North Dakota State Park Service
Rt. 2, Box 139
Mandan, N. Dak. 58554
(Write for list of parks with nature
    trails.)

OHIO

Lake Erie Junior Nature and
    Science Center
28728 Wolf Rd.
Bay Village, Ohio 44140

Hamilton County Park District
10245 Winton Rd.
Cincinnati, Ohio 45231
(Write for list of nature preserves
    and programs.)

Public Recreation Commission
222 E. Central Parkway
Cincinnati, Ohio 45202
(Write for list of outdoor education
    centers.)

Zoological Society of Cincinnati
3400 Vine St.
Cincinnati, Ohio 45220

The Cleveland Museum of Natural
    History
Wade Oval
University Circle
Cleveland, Ohio 44106

Center of Science and Industry
280 E. Broad St.
Columbus, Ohio 43215

Columbus Metropolitan Park Board
1251 E. Broad St.
Columbus, Ohio 43205
(Write for list of parks and
    programs.)

The Community Camp
137 E. State St.
Columbus, Ohio 43215

Aullwood Audubon Center
1000 Aullwood Rd.
Dayton, Ohio 45414

Outdoor Education
Mansfield City Schools
270 W. 6th St.
Mansfield, Ohio 44901

Park and Recreation Department
3760 Darrow Rd.
Stow, Ohio 44224

Toledo Zoological Society
2700 Broadway
Toledo, Ohio 43609

Ford Nature Education Center
Mill Creek Park
816 Glenwood Ave.
Youngstown, Ohio 44502

OKLAHOMA

Oklahoma City Zoo
Rt. 1, Box 478
Oklahoma City, Okla. 73111

Travertine Nature Center
Platt National Park
Box 201
Sulphur, Okla. 73086

Mohawk Park Zoo
5701 E. 36th St. N.
Tulsa, Okla. 74115

OREGON

Crater Lake National Park
Crater Lake, Oreg. 97604

Jewell Wildlife Meadows
Jewell, Oreg. 97126

Moore Park
Klamath Falls, Oreg. 97601

Oregon Humane Society
1067 N.E. Columbia Blvd.
Box 11364
Portland, Oreg. 97211

Oregon Museum of Science and
    Industry
4015 S.W. Canyon Rd.
Portland, Oreg. 97221

Portland Children's Museum
3037 S.W. 2nd Ave.
Portland, Oreg. 97201

Portland Zoological Gardens
4001 S.W. Canyon Rd.
Portland, Oreg. 97221

PENNSYLVANIA

Bucks County Department of Parks
    and Recreation
Administration Building
Doylestown, Pa. 18901
(Write for list of nature centers and
    programs.)

Hawk Mountain Sanctuary
    Association
Rt. 2
Kempton, Pa. 19529

The Academy of Natural Sciences
19th and The Parkway
Philadelphia, Pa. 19103

The Franklin Institute
Benjamin Franklin Parkway at 20th
    St.
Philadelphia, Pa. 19103

The Pennsylvania SPCA
350 E. Erie Ave.
Philadelphia, Pa. 19134

Schuylkill Valley Nature Center for
    Environmental Sciences
Hagy's Mill Rd.
Philadelphia, Pa. 19128

Wagner Free Institute of Science
Montgomery Ave. and 17th St.
Philadelphia, Pa. 19121

Reading Nature Center
Hill Rd. near Antietam Lake
Mail to: City Hall
Reading, Pa. 19601

The Reading Public Museum and
    Art Gallery
500 Museum Rd.
Reading, Pa. 19602

Everhart Museum
Nay Aug Park
Scranton, Pa. 18510

Allegheny National Forest
Warren, Pa. 16365

RHODE ISLAND

Kimball Bird Sanctuary
Burlingame State Park
Watchaug Pond
Charlestown, R.I. 02813

Dame Farm
Johnston, R.I. 02919

Norman Bird Sanctuary
  (Audubon Society)
Third Beach Rd.
Middletown, R.I. 02840

R.I. Development Council
Roger Williams Bldg.
Providence, R.I. 02908
(Write for information.)

SOUTH CAROLINA

The Charleston Museum
121 Rutledge Ave.
Charleston, S.C. 24901

Jim Fowler
The Animal Forest
1500 Old Town Rd.
Charlestowne Landing
Charleston, S.C. 29407

Columbia Zoological Park
Riverbanks Park
Box 1143
Columbia, S.C. 29202

SOUTH DAKOTA

Wind Cave National Park
Hot Springs, S. Dak. 57747

Department of Game, Fish, and
  Parks
Pierre, S. Dak. 57501
(Write for list of parks with
  trails.)

TENNESSEE

Andrew Jackson School Children's
  Museum
Jackson St.
Kingsport, Tenn. 37660

Bays Mountain Park Nature Center
Rt. 4
Kingsport, Tenn. 37660

Students' Museum, Inc.
3816 Oakland Dr.
Knoxville, Tenn. 37918

Boys' Clubs of Memphis, Inc.
189 S. Barksdale
Memphis, Tenn. 38104

Memphis Pink Palace Museum
232 Tilton Rd. at Central Ave.
Memphis, Tenn. 38111

Overton Park Zoo and Aquarium
Memphis, Tenn. 38112

Meeman Museum and Nature
  Center
Meeman–Shelby Forest State Park
Millington, Tenn. 38053

The Children's Museum
Bass and Ridley Sts.
Box 7067
Nashville, Tenn. 37210

Outdoor and Environmental
  Education
Metropolitan Nashville–Davidson
  County Schools
Howard St. and 2nd Ave.
Nashville, Tenn. 37204

Nature Center
Fall Creek Falls State Park
Pikeville, Tenn. 37367

Maryville College Environmental
  Education Center at Tremont
Townsend, Tenn. 37882

TEXAS

Natural Science Center
401 Deep Eddy Ave.
Austin, Tex. 78703

Junior Museum of Natural History
Box 3427
Bryan, Tex. 77801

Corpus Christi Museum
1919 N. Water St.
Corpus Christi, Tex. 78401

Dallas Museum of Natural History
Box 26193
Fair Park Station
Dallas, Tex. 75226

Fort Worth Museum of Science and
  History
1501 Montgomery St.
Fort Worth, Tex. 76107

Fort Worth Zoological Park
2727 Zoological Park Dr.
Fort Worth, Tex. 76110

Houston Museum of Natural
  Science
Box 8175
5800 Caroline St. in Hermann Park
Houston, Tex. 77004

Houston Zoological Gardens
#1 Zoo Circle Dr.
Houston, Tex. 77002

Prairie Dog Town
Box 2000, City Hall
Lubbock, Tex. 79549

Heard Natural Science Museum
  and Wildlife Sanctuary
Rt. 2
McKinney, Tex. 75069

The Humane Society of
  Nacogdoches County
1703 North St.
Nacogdoches, Tex. 75961

Strecker Museum
Baylor University
Waco, Tex. 76703

UTAH

The Humane Society of the U.S.
Rocky Mountain Regional Office
455 E. 4th South
Salt Lake City, Utah 84111

The Humane Society of Utah
4613 South 4000 West
Salt Lake City, Utah 84119

VERMONT

Green Mountain Audubon Nature
  Center
Huntington, Vt. 05462

The Merck Forest
Rupert, Vt. 05768

Fairbanks Museum and
  Planetarium
St. Johnsbury, Vt. 05819

Vermont Humane Society
Springfield, Vt. 05156

Conservation Society of Southern
  Vermont
Townshend, Vt. 05353

Vermont Institute of Natural
  Science
Woodstock, Vt. 05091

VIRGINIA

Va. Federation of Humane Societies
910 S. Payne St.
Alexandria, Va. 22314

Gulf Branch Nature Center
3608 N. Military Rd.
Arlington, Va. 22207

American Horse Protection
Association
629 River Bend Rd.
Great Falls, Va. 22066

George Washington National Forest
Massanutten Center
Harrisonburg, Va. 22801

Shenandoah National Park
Luray, Va. 22835
(Write for information on National
Environmental Study Areas and
other nature programs.)

Department of Conservation and
Economic Development
Division of Parks
1201 State Office Bldg.
Richmond, Va. 23219
(Write for list of nature centers.)

KIND
The National Humane Education
Center
Waterford, Va. 22190

WASHINGTON

Catherine Montgomery Interpretive
Center
Federation Forest State Park
Enumclaw, Wash. 98022

Olympic National Park
600 E. Park Ave.
Port Angeles, Wash. 98362

Cispus Environmental Center
Gifford Pinchot National Forest
Rt. 4
Randle, Wash. 98377

WEST VIRGINIA

The Children's Museum and
Planetarium at "Sunrise"
746 Myrtle Rd.
Charleston, W. Va. 25314

Monongahela National Forest
Elkins, W. Va. 26241

Oglebay Institute
Oglebay Park
Wheeling, W. Va. 26003

Oglebay Park Zoo
Oglebay Park
Wheeling, W. Va. 26003

WISCONSIN

Environmental Education Program
Madison Public Schools
Madison, Wis. 53703

Milwaukee Public Museum
800 W. Wells St.
Milwaukee, Wis. 53233

Schlitz Audubon Center
1111 E. Brown Deer Rd.
Milwaukee, Wis. 53217

Wisconsin Humane Society
4151 N. Humboldt Ave.
Milwaukee, Wis. 53212

Riveredge Nature Center, Inc.
4311 W. Hawthorne Dr.
Newburg, Wis. 53060

WYOMING

Casper Humane Society
103 Crescent Dr.

Mt. View Addition
Casper, Wyo. 82601

Devils Tower National Monument
Devils Tower, Wyo. 82714

National Elk Refuge
Jackson, Wyo. 83001

Teton Science School
Box 1111
Jackson, Wyo. 83001

Conservation Center for Creative
  Learning
863 Sweetwater St.
Lander, Wyo. 82520

PUERTO RICO

Bosque Nacional del Caribe
Box AQ
Rio Piedras, P.R. 00928